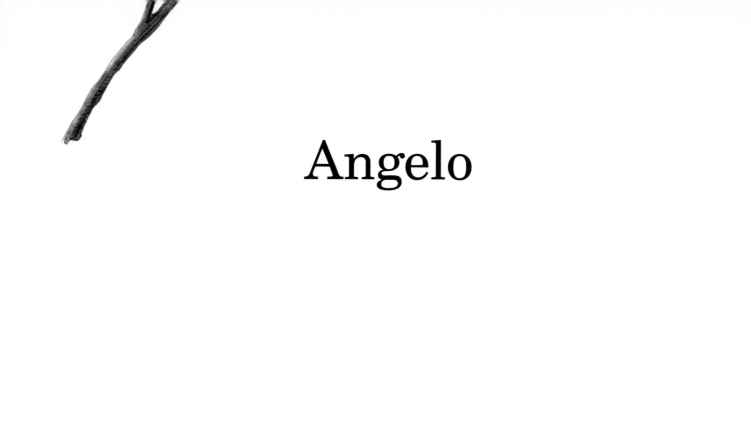

Angelo

For Ruthie

Library of Congress
Cataloging-in-Publication
Macaulay, David.
Angelo / David Macaulay
p. cm.
"Walter Lorraine Books."
Summary: While restoring the front of a church, an old master plasterer rescues an injured pigeon and nurses her back to health.
ISBN 0-618-16826-5
[1. Architecture — Conservation and restoration — Fiction. 2. Pigeons — Fiction. 3. Wildlife rescue — Fiction.]

PZ7.M1197 An 2002
[Fic] — dc21

2001039536

Printed in the United States of America
BVG 10 9 8 7 6 5 4 3 2 1

Angelo

David Macaulay

Houghton Mifflin Company Boston 2002

Walter Lorraine 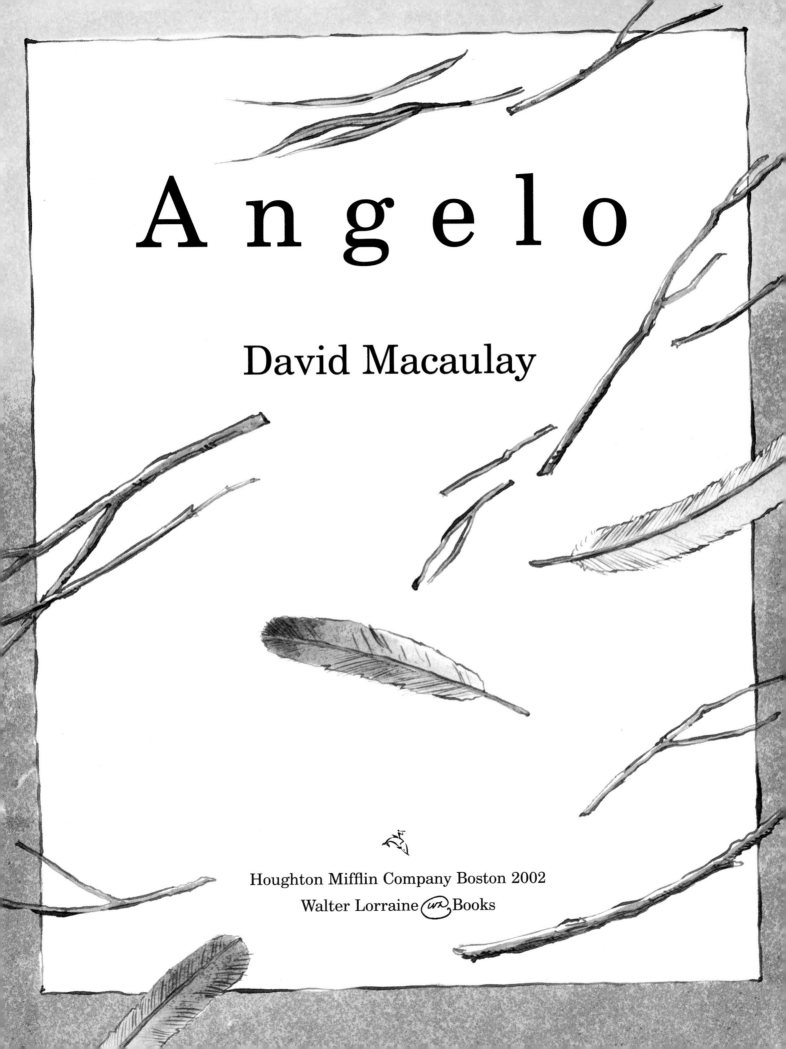 Books

As Angelo cleared away the tangle of sticks and feathers left along the ledges of the old church by generations of thoughtless pigeons, he peered into every nook and cranny looking for cracks. They would all have to be repaired before he could apply a new coat of stucco.

At first he mistook her for just another abandoned nest. "What's this?" He moved in for a closer look. She was small, barely breathing.

"What are you doing here?" He tried coaxing her with the end of his broom.

"Come on. You can't stay there. I've got work to do." But she did stay there, so he worked around her.

At the end of the day, he scooped the helpless creature up in his hat and set off for home, hoping to find someplace to leave her along the way. He was still carrying her when he reached his own front door.

"Okay. Just one night," he grumbled. "But you sleep
on the terrace."

When he noticed a large cat cleaning its paws on a
nearby roof, he brought her back into the apartment.

"Mamma mia! I restore walls, not pigeons."

He continued complaining as he made her bed.

In spite of the demands of his work, not to mention his professional dislike for pigeons, Angelo soon found himself devoting all his spare time to her recovery.

When she was strong enough, he started taking her to work.

On sunny weekends he drove her out into the countryside to recuperate among the ancient ruins and majestic pines.

In the evenings, he introduced her to his favorite music.

With this kind of attention, it wasn't long before she was completely recovered. One morning after breakfast, as he left for the church, she disappeared over the rooftops.

16

Angelo loved his work. With wet plaster and a few
simple tools, he had spent his whole life making
crumbling walls smooth again and bringing even the
most weathered pieces of sculpture back to life.

She was just beginning her career in the performing arts—as an actress in one of the more popular piazzas.

From time to time, she would stop by and watch Angelo work. After a few months she realized that he was slowing down. It was taking him longer to mix the stucco and he seemed to be resting more often.

One afternoon, she paid him a visit. The old man looked
tired and worried and at first he didn't recognize her.
Then she cooed.

"Hey. Is that you, Bird? I suppose you want your ledge
back, eh?"

She cooed again.

"Well, I'll tell you. I don't know whether this wall is
getting bigger or I'm getting smaller but I'm starting to
wonder if I'll ever see it finished."

Shaking his head, he picked up a small brush and went
back to cleaning between the toes of an evangelist. She
stayed with him for the rest of the afternoon to coo
encouragement. So he worked around her.

She showed up again the following day and every day
after that to help. As the temperature rose, she fanned
him with her wings. When he looked particularly weary,
she carried his handkerchief to a nearby fountain and
soaked it in the cool water. From time to time, Angelo
would interrupt his work to explain some of the finer
points of his craft.

At lunchtime, she and a few friends provided
entertainment. The longer Angelo sat and rested, the
better he would work in the afternoons.
Also, the more crumbs he dropped.

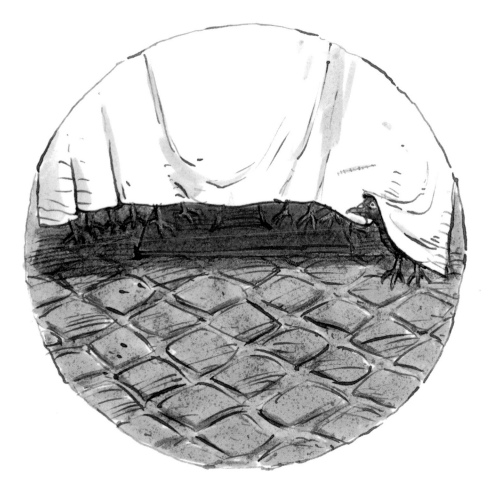

Even with her help, however, there still didn't seem to
be enough hours in the day. Before long, they were
working right through lunch.

Fortunately, they had their weekends to rest. One
Saturday, while heading out to the countryside,
Angelo made an announcement.
"My friend, it is time you had a name and I have been
giving the matter considerable thought. Since I found
you on a Wednesday, I have decided to call you
'Wednesday.'
"'M-e-r-c-o-l-e-d-i,' " he said slowly and proudly.
His suggestion was greeted with absolute silence.
"Okay. How about Sylvia?"

That evening as Sylvia happily pecked her pasta,
Angelo spoke at great length of his life, his career and
his hope that this church would be his crowning
achievement.

Week after week, month after month, the pair toiled side by side. The heat of summer gradually gave way to the cool winds of autumn and ultimately to the chill of winter. Some days were just too cold for mixing stucco.

34

After more than two years of grueling work, the end was at last in sight. But so too was another winter and Angelo was now moving very slowly. In order to finish before the cold weather returned, they gave up their much-loved visits to the countryside.

It was a warm November afternoon when Angelo finally applied the last coat of stucco to the cherubs in the high pediment. With a single confident stroke of the trowel, his work at last was complete.

To Sylvia's surprise, however, he now seemed more worried than ever. At dinner that evening, she did everything she could to cheer him up. But, the harder she tried, the more he just stared into his linguini. Finally, after a long silence, he spoke.

"Plasterers don't live forever, you know. This place has become your home. Where will you go when I'm gone? How will I know you're safe?"

He continued staring at his linguini until suddenly:
"Of course! That's it!"
He grabbed his hat and coat and a flashlight.
"Wait here, Sylvia."

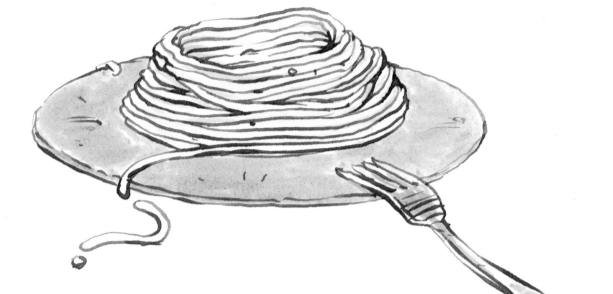

The sun was just beginning to rise when Angelo
eventually returned. He was exhausted and looked
older than ever. But as they fell into their favorite
chair, she saw that for the first time in months he was
happy. That afternoon, workers began removing the
scaffolding from the front of the church.

When Angelo didn't show up to see his work revealed, the men knew something was wrong.

They found him lying on his bed surrounded by a tangle of sticks and feathers.

The day Angelo was carried into the church, every detail of the old building looked like new. Only one of them truly was.

Far above the street and between the cherubs sat a perfect single-family nest. To make sure that it could never be swept away, Angelo had shaped every stick and every feather of Sylvia's new home out of stucco. From it she could easily see beyond the rooftops and domes of the city to the distant countryside with its ancient tombs and majestic pines.

Many years later, when the church once again required
some attention, a pair of young plasterers came upon
Angelo's beautiful nest. It was still in perfect condition.
In the nest were a few feathers and what appeared to
be the remains of an old hat.
Neither plasterer touched a thing.